MONEYWISE

WHAT is MONEY?

Nancy Dickmann

BROWN BEAR BOOKS

Published by Brown Bear Books Ltd
4877 N. Circulo Bujia
Tucson, AZ 85718
USA

and

Studio G14, Regent Studios,
1 Thane Villas, London N7 7PH, UK

ISBN 978-1-78121-925-6 (library bound)
ISBN 978-1-78121-931-7 (paperback)

Library of Congress Cataloging-in-Publication Data available on request

Text: Nancy Dickmann
Designer: Trudi Webb
Design Manager: Keith Davis
Children's Publisher: Anne O'Daly

Manufactured in the United States of America
CPSIA compliance information: Batch#AG/PO 5656

Picture Credits
The photographs in this book are used by permission and through the courtesy of:

Cover: Keith Davisi; Interior: Alamy: Heritage Image Partnership Ltd 8-9; iStock: vm 4-5; Shutterstock: Dragon Images 12–13, Juliek2 14–15, KreativKolors 10–11, Rido 18–19, Marina Varnava 6–7, Zefart 16–17, Drazen Zigic 20–21.

All other artwork and photography
© Brown Bear Books.

t-top, r-right, l-left, c-center, b-bottom

Brown Bear Books has made every attempt to contact the copyright holder. If you have any information about omissions please contact: licensing@brownbearbooks.co.uk

Websites
The website addresses in this book were valid at the time of going to press. However, it is possible that contents or addresses may change following publication of this book. No responsibility for any such changes can be accepted by the author or the publisher. Readers should be supervised when they access the Internet.

Words in **bold** appear in the Words to Know on page 23

Contents

Buying and SELLING

What do you like to buy? How do you pay for it?

Maybe you like to spend your allowance on candy or craft supplies. Chances are, when you buy something, you use money to pay for it. Money comes in different forms. They all have a value that everyone agrees on.

Stores, cafes, and online retailers all accept money as payment.

Money Everywhere

Many adults use money every day. They might buy a coffee on the way to work, or fill up their car with gas. They use money to pay for rent, electricity, and groceries. People sometimes say that "money makes the world go around." And they're probably right!

Our word "money" comes from an old name for the Roman goddess Juno. There was a temple to Juno near the place where the Romans made their coins.

How it BEGAN

Humans didn't always use money. Instead, they traded for what they needed.

Imagine that a farmer needed a new tool. He could trade with the **blacksmith** for it. He might offer a sack of wheat or a chicken. He could even offer his labor, promising to plow a field. This is called **barter**. Humans have used it for thousands of years.

Barter only works if you have something that the person you're trading with wants.

Making Things Simpler

Some people started trading things like animal skins, salt, or grain. These were goods that lots of people wanted. Even if you didn't need them yourself, you could trade them for something that you did need. Eventually, people began trading metal coins instead.

MONEY QUESTION

People sometimes use barter today. Can you think of a time when you have used it? Have you ever swapped toys or trading cards with a friend?

In the PAST

People have been using metal coins for thousands of years.

Early coins were often made from gold or silver, or a mix of the two. The coins of each type were identical in size and weight. They were stamped with pictures such as animals or the heads of kings. Coins were small and **portable**—perfect for trading.

People often find coins from the past that have been hidden or buried.

MONEY QUESTION

Imagine that you need to invent a new kind of money to replace coins. What would you use? How much would it be worth?

Beads and Bones

Not everyone used metal coins. Some groups used small shells as money, and others used wampum—strings of beads made from shells. Bones and feathers have also been used as money. One group on the Pacific island of Yap uses huge stone disks!

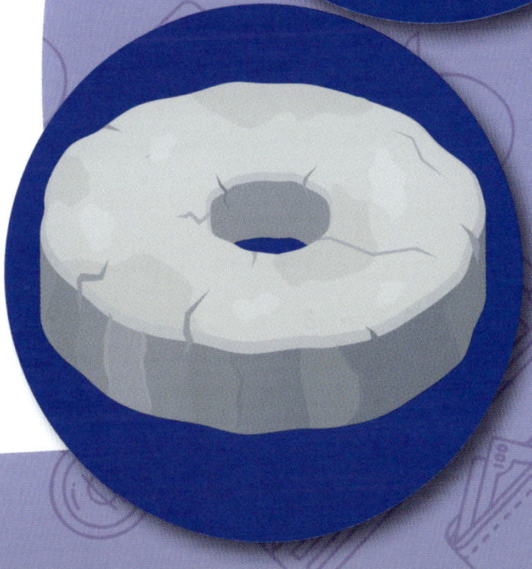

Coins and NOTES

Money that you can hold in your hand is called cash.

Coins are no longer made of gold or silver. They are made from copper, nickel, and zinc. These metals are less valuable. The metals in most coins are worth much less than the value of the coin. Even so, a bag of coins is still heavy to carry around. Paper is lighter.

Most coins today are round, but some come in other shapes such as squares.

MONEY TIP

Gold coins were valuable because gold is expensive. But a piece of paper is very cheap. A banknote only has value because people agree that it does.

Swap coins for banknote

Banknotes

Paper money first appeared in China nearly 1,500 years ago. In Europe, it wasn't used until hundreds of years later. These early paper notes were **receipts** for coins deposited at a **bank**. They could be traded for coins again. Today, some countries make **banknotes** out of plastic.

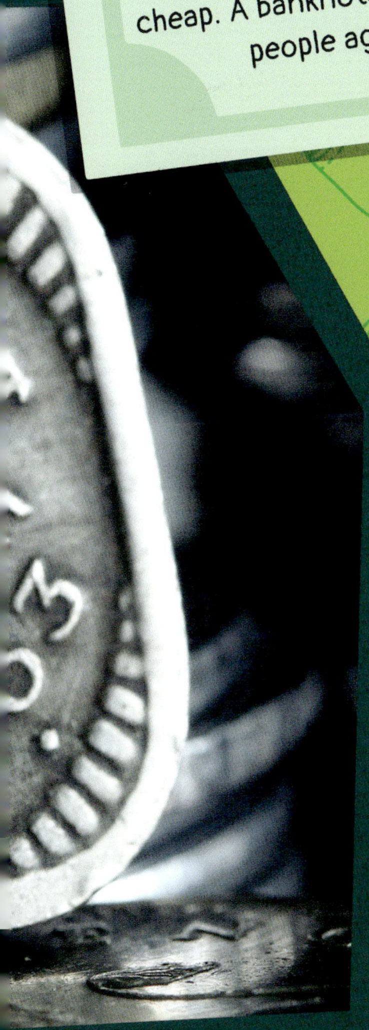

Dollars and CENTS

People sometimes call U.S. banknotes "greenbacks." This is because during the 1800s, some banknotes were printed in green ink.

When you spend money, you do it in dollars and cents.

Currency is a word for a particular country's system of money. In the United States, the currency is the dollar. A dollar is divided into 100 cents. We have banknotes for dollar amounts and coins for cents. There are also one-dollar coins.

Our word "dollar" comes from an old German coin known as a taler.

American coins and notes show national symbols and important people.

History of the Dollar

The United States used to be part of the United Kingdom. Its people used British, Spanish, and French money. But in the 1770s, the U.S. fought for independence. Its leaders wanted the new country to have its own currency. They started making coins in 1792.

Around the WORLD

Foreign notes and coins often show a country's leaders, landmarks, or wildlife.

Every country uses money, but each one has its own currency.

Some countries, such as Canada, have their own version of the dollar. It's not worth the same as a U.S. dollar. In Mexico, they use the peso. The United Kingdom has the pound, and in Japan it's the yen. Many countries in Europe share the same currency, called the euro.

MONEY TIP

People sometimes bring foreign coins home from vacation. You could use them to start a collection, or find a charity that collects them to cash in and help others.

Changing Money

When you visit another country, you can't usually spend dollars. You need to use that country's currency instead. You can trade your money for the currency you need. Each currency has its own value. A bank will calculate how much you get for your dollars.

Banks and MINTS

We rely on banks to take care of our money.

You've probably been to a local bank. They make **loans** and take care of customers' money. Most countries also have a central bank. It is usually linked to the government. A central bank manages the country's currency. It controls the amount of money there is.

A large factory can print millions of banknotes every day.

Money can get worn or torn when it gets used. The average five-dollar bill lasts five years before it's too worn to use anymore. Coins last longer—about 30 years.

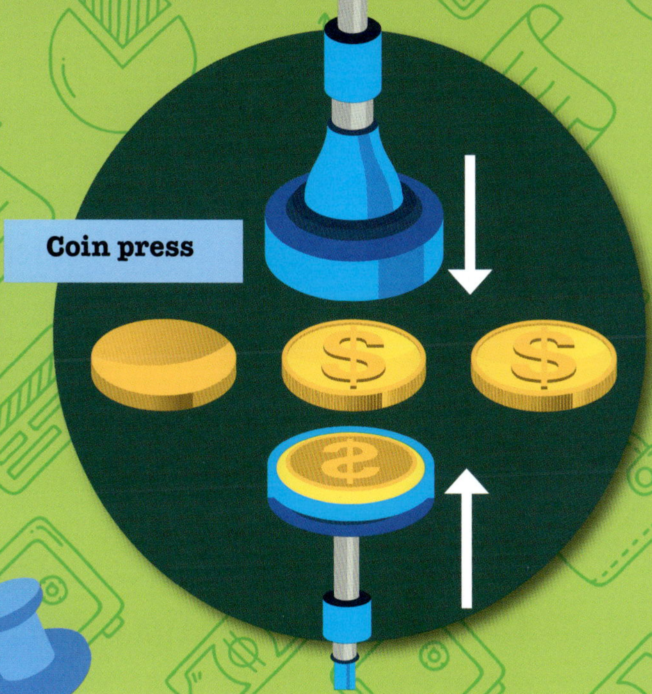

Making Money

A mint is a factory that makes coins. A coin starts as a blank metal disk. A machine presses pictures and words onto it. Different factories print banknotes. The notes use special paper and ink. It is harder for criminals to make fake versions of these materials.

Moving ONLINE

Cash is very useful, but there are other ways to spend.

Have you ever seen someone tap their card or phone on a reader to pay? Or type in their card number to buy something online? These are modern, convenient ways of paying. You don't need to hand over coins or notes. But you are still spending money!

If you want to use your phone to pay, you'll need a banking app.

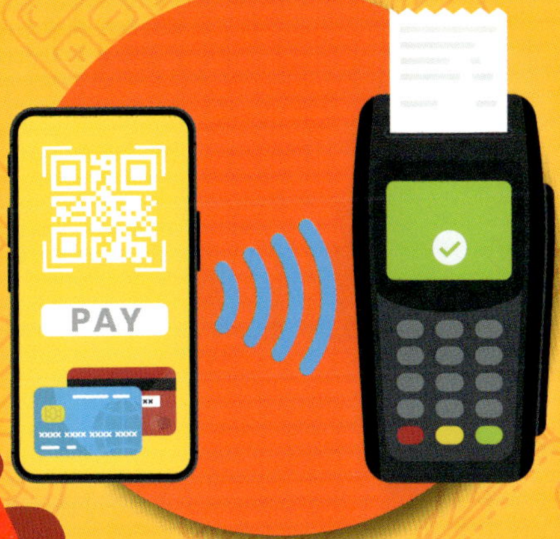

Keeping Track

When you tap to pay or shop online, the money comes out of your **bank account**. The bank's computer system keeps track of how much money is in each account. When you spend, it updates the amount. This is money in the form of numbers, not coins or notes.

MONEY QUESTION

When you are out shopping, do you see more people paying with cash, or with phones or cards? Why do you think people choose each method?

The Future OF MONEY

We've come a long way from the days of trading seashells and gold coins.

In the past, all money was created by governments or central banks. Some new currencies are created by computer networks. They are called **crypto-currencies**. These currencies are digital only. They don't exist as coins or notes. They can be used around the world.

During the Covid pandemic, many people stopped using cash, to avoid passing on germs.

Changing Habits

Money has changed a lot. So has the way we use it. Just fifty years ago, most payments were made in cash. But in recent years people have stopped using cash as often. They are using cards and payment apps more than before. Who knows how we'll pay in the future?

MONEY TIP

No matter how you pay, you can save money by managing it well. Talk to an adult for advice on making a spending and saving plan.

Use Your Skills!

It's time to test out your money knowledge! You can check your answers on page 24.

1 Can you name two objects that were used as money in the past?

2 Charlotte's family is going on vacation to Mexico. What kind of money will they spend?

3 Where are coins made?

Find out More

Websites

kids.britannica.com/kids/article/money/399548

www.coolkidfacts.com/money-for-kids/

www.usmint.gov/learn/kids/coins-life

Books

Reina, Mary. **Spend Money.** Mankato, Minn.: Capstone Press, 2020.

Schuh, Mari. **Money Around the World** (Money and Me). Vero Beach, Fla.: Rourke Educational Media, 2019.

Sherman, Jill. **Money: What You Need to Know.** Mankato, Minn.: Capstone Press, 2018.

Words to Know

app a piece of software that lets a device, such as a smartphone, do a specific task

bank a business that makes loans and manages its customers' money

bank account an arrangement with a bank so that they can take care of your money

banknote a piece of foldable money made from paper or sometimes plastic

barter a system where people trade goods or services instead of paying with money

blacksmith a person who makes tools and other objects from iron or steel by heating and hammering the metal

cash money in the form of coins or paper notes

crypto-currency a type of digital currency that is created by a computer network

currency the system of money used in a particular country, for example the dollar or peso

loan money that a person or business borrows, often from a bank, which must be paid back with interest

portable small, light, and easy to carry around

receipt a slip of paper given in return for money or goods, which can be used as proof of the transaction

Index

Answers

1. Choose two from: metal coins; seashells; strings of beads; bones; feathers; large stone disks.
2. The currency in Mexico is the peso, so Charlotte's family will pay for things in pesos.
3. Coins are made at a special kind of factory called a mint.